WHY WAR HAPPENED

WHAT CAUSED THE CIVIL WAR?

BY ROBYN HARDYMAN

Gareth Stevens PUBLISHING

Please visit our website, www.garethstevens.com.
For a free color catalog of all our high-quality books,
call toll free 1-800-542-2595 or fax 1-877-542-2596.

Cataloging-in-Publication Data
Names: Hardyman, Robyn.
Title: What caused the Civil War? / Robyn Hardyman.
Description: New York : Gareth Stevens Publishing, 2017. | Series: Why war happened | Includes index.
Identifiers: ISBN 9781482451863 (pbk.) | ISBN 9781482451801 (library bound) | ISBN 9781482452044 (6 pack)
Subjects: LCSH: United States--History--Civil War, 1861-1865--Juvenile literature. | United States--History--Civil War, 1861-1865--Causes--Juvenile literature.
Classification: LCC E468.H37 2017 | DDC 973.7--dc23

First Edition

Published in 2017 by
Gareth Stevens Publishing
111 East 14th Street, Suite 349
New York, NY 10003

Produced by Calcium
Editors: Sarah Eason and Harriet McGregor
Designer: Simon Borrough
Picture researcher: Rachel Blount

Picture credits: Cover: Getty: John Parrot/Stocktrek Images (painting), Shutterstock: kasha_malasha (bkgrd). Inside: Library of Congress: 17, Leffler, Warren K 44, Lindsley, H. B 15, Rees Print & Litho. Company 29; Shutterstock: Everett Historical 5, 6, 7, 9, 11, 12, 13, 14, 20, 21, 28, 30, 31, 33, 35, 36, 39, 41, 43, Everett Historical/portrait by Alexander Gardner 23, Everett Historical/Andrew J. Russell 19, Jiri Flogel 26, Rainer Lesniewski 24, Anne Power 8.

Printed in the United States of America
CPSIA compliance information: Batch #CS16GS: For further information contact Gareth Stevens, New York, New York at 1-800-542-2595.

CONTENTS

Words in the glossary appear in **bold** type
the first time they are used in the text.

CHAPTER 1

THE CIVIL WAR

The Civil War was fought in the United States between 1861 and 1865. It is sometimes called "The War Between the States" because it was fought between 11 states in the South of the country and the Northern states. A **civil war** is one that is fought between two sides from the same country, rather than two sides from different countries.

The Southern states wanted to leave the union of the United States of America. They formed their own group called the Confederate States of America, and wanted to be a separate country. They did not want the U.S. government to tell them what to do or to make laws they did not agree with. They chose Jefferson Davis (1808–1889) as their President. The U.S. government and the states that remained loyal to it were called the Union.

There were many causes of the war, but they were all the result of the differences between the Southern and Northern states. The two areas had very different ways of life, different traditions, economies, and cultures. The way that the United States was governed meant that these differences caused problems. Ever since the **U.S. Constitution** first came into effect in 1789, there had been arguments about how much power the states should have, and how much should be controlled by the central federal government. By the 1850s, the Southern states thought that the federal government was taking away too many of their powers.

A Union Army regiment of African American soldiers fought bravely at the attack on Fort Wagner in 1863.

The Civil War was long and terrible. It was the bloodiest war in U.S. history. About 650,000 people were killed, and about 210,000 of these people were soldiers. More than half of the deaths during the war were the result of disease, because medicine was very poor in those days.

AN UNEQUAL FIGHT

The Union Army was almost twice as big as the Confederate Army. The Union had just over 2 million soldiers, while the Confederates had just over 1 million. One-third of all white men in the South aged between 18 and 40 died in the war.

NORTH AND SOUTH

In the mid-1800s, life in the Southern states was very different from life in the Northern states. People earned their livings in different ways, and they also had different ideas about politics and personal freedoms.

In the South, the **economy** was based on farming and **agriculture**. Important crops such as tobacco, sugar cane, and cotton grew well in the warm Southern climate. They created wealth for farmers in these states. Small farms were run by families who worked the land themselves. The larger farms were called **plantations**, and the labor force for these was usually made up of **slaves**. These were workers who were bought for money by the plantation owners, and became their property. They were not free to leave the plantations, and had to work according to the rules laid down by their owners. Slaves were almost all African men and women who had been shipped over from West Africa by merchants, who sold them in markets to landowners.

Bales of cotton were shipped out from the South to the North of the country and to countries overseas.

George Washington (1732–1799), the first President of the United States, was a plantation owner and had slaves on his estate.

In the North, the climate did not suit the cultivation of cotton and tobacco. There they had natural **resources** such as coal, and during the nineteenth century, new industries began to develop, such as coal mining and steel manufacturing. Factories were built and workers moved to the towns to work in them. The towns grew rapidly into urban centers. Workers there were free, not slaves, and they were paid wages. Many of the lowest-paid jobs were done by **immigrants** from Europe who had recently arrived in America. Other new jobs were also created, to run these businesses and to keep the new cities working. These included jobs in transportation, healthcare, law, and construction. There were more schools in the North than in the South, and standards of education were generally higher.

CITY LIFE

By 1860, one-quarter of people in the North were living in large cities. The boom in manufacturing was helped by the growth in the transportation network, especially the railroads. Raw materials and finished goods could be transported more easily in the North.

PLANTATION OR CITY

Life on a Southern plantation was very different from life in a Northern city. For the slaves it was endless hard work, while the white owners and managers lived lives of great comfort. In the North, people lived in smaller homes and did different jobs.

After 1800, cotton plantations spread across a huge stretch of the South. The other main crop was sugar. Society in the South had clear class divisions. At the top were a lucky few, the big landowners of the large plantations. They grew rich from their crops and built large homes for themselves. They often built in the style of their original homeland, such as in English or Spanish colonial style.

Most people, however, lived much more modestly. They were farmers on a smaller scale. They mostly owned their own land, and worked it themselves. There were few cities in the South, and the road network was poor. There were not many schools, and children received little education. About half of the population in the South was slaves. In 1860, there were about 4 million slaves.

The richest landowners in the South built themselves huge mansions like this one.

All five generations of this slave family were born on the same plantation in South Carolina, but it was rare for families to be able to stay together in this way.

In the Northern cities, even the poorest were free. They could work for wages and move freely from place to place. Living conditions were not always good, however, as the cities grew fast and services such as water and energy did not grow at a pace to keep up. There was more education in the cities, and this gave people the opportunity to learn and find better jobs. People had the chance to improve their standard of living if they worked hard. There were increasing numbers of jobs in trade and business.

IMMIGRATION FROM IRELAND

A Great Famine in Ireland in 1845–1850 made many Irish people leave their homeland and travel to the United States, looking for a place to make a better life. By 1850, one-quarter of the people living in New York City, for example, were Irish. This was the largest city in the country.

CHAPTER 2

SLAVERY

By the middle of the 1800s, the United States had been an independent country for less than 100 years. The country was growing rapidly, expanding to the west, and people disagreed on issues about the way the country should be run. One of the most important of those issues was slavery.

By 1860, there were 4 million slaves in the South, and this was nearly the same size as the white population. About 60 percent of them worked on the plantations, growing cotton. The other main crop in the South was sugar. Working this crop was the hardest work of all, and the slaves worked in gangs. Even the children of slaves were put to work, and the old. The sugar crop took six months to harvest and it was very hard, unpleasant work.

Slaves did a variety of jobs on the plantation. Many worked out in the fields, doing the backbreaking work. The most experienced laborers were allowed to make decisions about the crop, such as when to pick and how to pack and transport it. Others had particular skills, such as masons, joiners, and metalworkers, and the plantations needed them, too. The women often worked as nurses, cooks, and seamstresses. Within the homes of the owners and managers, many domestic slaves served the family.

Most slaves lived in poor conditions, in small houses near the fields. Domestic slaves lived at the main house, in small rooms above the kitchen or in the stables. All slaves could be bought or sold at any time, and families could be broken up. Children were often sold as soon as they were old enough to work, and never saw their parents again.

BUYING AND SELLING

Slaves were bought and sold in markets, like other goods. Slave dealers set up in business in the South. This image shows the premises of a slave dealer, with their slave pen on the right. Slaves like this woman were held here while they waited to be sold to a new owner.

HISTORY OF THE SLAVE TRADE

Slavery had been common in the Southern states since the late 1600s. As the need for manual labor grew, it became harder and more expensive to find workers to do the tough jobs in the cotton, tobacco, and sugar cane fields. More and more Africans were taken from their homes in West Africa, shipped across the Atlantic and sold into slavery. In the early 1700s, new laws established the rights of slave owners and the status of slaves.

Owning slaves became a sign of wealth in the South, where the agricultural economy depended on them as a labor force. In the North, however, the economy no longer relied so much on agriculture and slaves were not needed. Slavery had once existed there also, but it had almost died out by the 1850s. Some people in the North had begun to oppose slavery. These people were known as **abolitionists**. They wanted slavery to be abolished, or made illegal, throughout the United States.

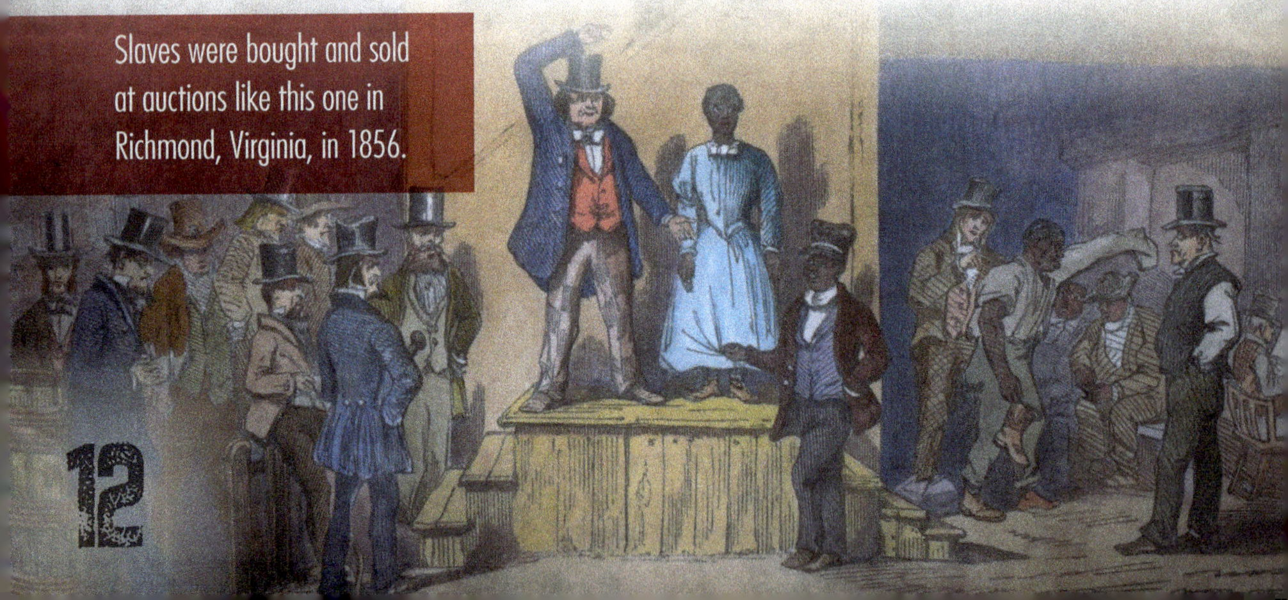

Slaves were bought and sold at auctions like this one in Richmond, Virginia, in 1856.

Over time, the voices of the abolitionists began to be heard more and more. This made people in the Southern states fearful that their way of life was under threat. Without slaves to do the work on the plantations, their economy would be in danger. They began to argue that slavery was not only necessary, but also good. They argued that it gave shelter and work to people who would otherwise not have them.

These slaves are using a cotton gin to process raw cotton and make it ready for the cotton mills.

THE COTTON GIN

In 1793, a Northerner named Eli Whitney (1765–1825) invented the cotton gin. This machine made it possible for the textile mills that made cloth to use the type of cotton crop that grew most easily in the South. Cotton became the main crop, and more slaves were needed to grow it.

THE UNDERGROUND RAILROAD

As Northern criticism of slavery grew, more slaves in the South began to try to escape. They headed for the Northern states or for Canada. Gradually, a network developed to try to help escaping slaves reach safety. This was called the Underground Railroad.

It was not a railroad, and it was not underground. It was called underground because it was secret, and its activities were usually carried out in darkness. It was called a railroad because it was a network of people and places. It used the language of the railroad to describe itself, so helpers were "conductors" and the people who were escaping were called "freight" or "packages," to keep the activity secret. The most active helpers on the Underground Railroad were black slaves who had already escaped. Abolitionists and other sympathetic white people also helped them.

This image shows fleeing slaves arriving in Philadelphia.

The Southern states were unhappy at the number of slaves escaping, and put pressure on the lawmakers in Washington, D.C., to stop it. In September 1850, a federal law was passed by Congress called the Fugitive Slave Act. This harsh law required all escaped slaves to be returned to their owners, even if they had reached free states. A similar law had existed since 1793, but it had not been strongly enforced. There was widespread opposition to the new law in the North, as it forced citizens to help capture runaway slaves. Resistance grew and some states, such as Vermont and Wisconsin, passed new measures to try to bypass it. The Underground Railroad grew stronger still, and activists forcibly liberated, or freed, some recaptured slaves from custody.

Public opinion in the North was turning decisively against slavery. In 1852, Harriet Beecher Stowe (1811–1896) wrote a very popular novel, *Uncle Tom's Cabin*, in which she challenged the Southern myth that black people were happy to be slaves.

HARRIET TUBMAN

Harriet Tubman (1822–1913) was a black slave who escaped from slavery in Maryland in 1849, leaving behind her husband and family. She returned to the South in secret at least 19 times, to help 300 more slaves to escape on the Underground Railroad.

ABOLITIONISTS

After the Fugitive Slave Act of 1850, abolitionists increased their efforts against slavery. Their aim was to achieve an immediate end to slavery, the **emancipation** of all slaves, and the end of racial **discrimination**. There were many key individuals who worked for the cause.

Several of these people were ex-slaves, who had escaped to freedom. One of them was Frederick Douglass (1818–1895). He was an escaped slave but he was also educated. He began to speak out at public meetings, about the terrible experience of being a slave. His speeches and his writings attracted wide support. He lived through the Civil War, and fought for the rights of black soldiers.

Sojourner Truth (c. 1797–1883) was another freed slave who campaigned for the abolition of slavery across the United States. She also championed the rights of women. She traveled the country telling people about the life of a slave, helping them understand that slavery was wrong and should be stopped.

It was not only black people who called for an end to slavery. Religious preachers in the North spoke out passionately against it. In 1833, the American Anti-Slavery Society had formed and it was very active in promoting its cause in the North. The cause attracted women, also, who linked the rights of slaves with the rights of women. Powerful speakers on the issue included Lucy Stone (1818–1893), Lucretia Mott (1793–1880), and Elizabeth Cady Stanton (1815–1902). Mott and Stanton launched the American women's rights movement in 1848. After the Civil War, they continued to work to support black people and women, and fight for their equal rights.

Abolitionists also supported equality in education. In higher education, abolitionists had founded Oberlin College, Ohio, in 1833, the nation's first mixed-race and mixed-gender college. Its first black student graduated in 1844.

Frederick Douglass advised President Lincoln on the treatment of black soldiers.

FREDERICK DOUGLASS

Frederick Douglass famously wrote about slavery:

"No man can put a chain about the ankle of his fellow man without at last finding the other end fastened about his own neck."

CHAPTER 3

A GROWING COUNTRY

During the first half of the 1800s, the United States grew quickly. It was expanding toward the West, taking over new territory and creating new states. This expansion raised the issue of whether the new states would permit slavery or make it illegal. It was therefore an important factor in the outbreak of the Civil War.

In 1803, the U.S. President bought the Louisiana Territory from France. This land west of the Mississippi almost doubled the size of the country. After war with Mexico in the 1840s, the country gained a huge area in the southwest, including Texas and California, and they gained the Oregon Territory from Britain. Settlers moved west to live in these new states.

The federal government was designed to represent its citizens fairly. The number of seats each state had in the House of Representatives depended on the size of its population. Each state had two representatives in the Senate. As new states were created, people feared that either those who supported slavery or those against it would have too much power in the government. In 1820, the number of states in which slavery was legal was the same as the number where it was not legal. To keep this balance, the Missouri **Compromise** was agreed in 1820. Missouri could join the United States as a slave state if Maine was allowed to join as a free state. It was only a matter of time, however, before this issue would become critical once again, as more states were added to the Union.

Soon, each new state became a battleground for power between the North that wanted slavery to be illegal and the South that supported slavery. The South saw its power slipping away.

THE TRANSCONTINENTAL RAILROAD

As the country expanded, the population grew from 5.2 million people in 1800, to 76.2 million in 1900. The railroad played an important part in connecting its huge regions across long distances. Talk of a Transcontinental Railroad began in the 1830s, and construction began in the 1860s.

The new railroad created an important link across the huge distances of the United States.

BLEEDING KANSAS

The balance of power in the new states held until 1854, when the Kansas-Nebraska Act became law. This Act allowed the people of these states to vote on whether or not slavery should be legal, and so replaced the Missouri Compromise.

People were deeply divided on this issue, and supporters of both sides flooded into the states. By late 1855, rival governments had been set up in Kansas, one backed by pro-slavery groups, the other by abolitionists. Soon, fighting broke out, and a period of violence followed that lasted for five years, up to the start of the Civil War. This period is known as Bleeding Kansas. In the end, the territories agreed on constitutions that did not allow slavery.

John Brown and his forces were trapped inside the engine house of the Harper's Ferry Armory by the marines outside.

John Brown

One active abolitionist during this fight was a white man, John Brown (1800–1859). He had been trying to help black people who had escaped from slavery, but he was frustrated at the slow progress being made. He was not against using violence to bring an end to such an evil practice. In 1859, John Brown put together a radical plan to arm the slaves in the South so that they could rise up against their masters. To do this he needed weapons, so in October he led a small group on a raid against a federal armory, at Harper's Ferry in Virginia. There were thousands of weapons there. At first they were successful, but soon they were surrounded by a group of U.S. marines. Brown was taken prisoner and in December he was hanged for **treason**. Although his action had not succeeded, his story became famous. It raised the profile of the subject of abolition and made agreement between the North and South almost impossible. It was therefore an important factor in contributing to the outbreak of the Civil War.

KANSAS CASUALTIES

During the Civil War, Kansas suffered more **casualties** than any other Union state, because it was so divided on the issue of slavery.

NEW PRESIDENT

In November 1860, the country held an election to find its new president. The winner of the election would be an important factor in determining whether or not a civil war could be avoided.

The Republican candidate was Abraham Lincoln (1809–1865). He and his party were firmly in favor of the Southern states remaining part of a united country. They were also opposed to slavery. Although they said they would allow slavery to continue in the South, they did not want it to be allowed in the new territories to the west. Lincoln had spoken out against slavery and won national recognition for his arguments.

The Democratic Party was divided on the issue of slavery, and broke into two parts, Northern and Southern. Turnout at the election was unusually high, more than 80 percent, because people held strong views on the issues of secession, or withdrawal from the Union, and slavery. The Republican Party was dominant in the North, and in the end they won the election. However, they did not win in a single state where slavery was still legal.

This was the final insult for the Southern states. They believed that Lincoln's election spelled the end of their way of life, and their culture that was based on the widespread use of slave labor. They saw that there would be nothing to stop the North imposing their views on the whole nation, and the South would have very little power. The new president would not be inaugurated until March 1861. Before that happened, they intended to advance plans to **secede** from the Union.

REPUBLICAN DETERMINATION

In the election campaign, the Republicans spoke out forcefully against the breakup of the Union of states:

> *"We denounce those threats of disunion . . . as denying the vital principles of a free government, and as an avowal of contemplated treason, which it is the imperative duty of an indignant people sternly to rebuke and forever silence."*

The South ignored this warning, and did not realize how far the North would go to hold the Union together.

Abraham Lincoln will always be remembered for preserving the Union during the Civil War and for bringing about the emancipation of slaves.

LAST CHANCE

The election of President Lincoln seemed to make secession inevitable, and end all hopes that a civil war could be avoided. There was so much at stake, however, that a last-minute effort was made to find a peaceful solution.

After the election, South Carolina immediately called a convention. On December 20, 1860, they voted to secede. This was the first state to leave the Union. The states of Mississippi, Florida, Alabama, Georgia, Louisiana, and Texas

This map shows which states did and did not allow slavery at the start of the war in 1861.

followed in January and February of 1861. They explained that the reason for their action was the movement to abolish slavery, and its influence on the politics of the North. They believed that their right to own slaves was written into the Constitution.

On February 4, 1861, these states agreed to form a new federal government, the Confederate States of America. Southerners resigned their seats in the Senate and the House of Representatives. In a last attempt to preserve the Union, some people had suggested a compromise in December, the Crittenden Compromise. This proposed banning slavery in the North but guaranteeing it in the South, but Lincoln and the Republicans rejected it. In February 1861, a Peace Conference was held in Washington, D.C. It proposed a solution similar to the Crittenden Compromise, but it was rejected by Congress. The Republicans proposed an alternative compromise: slavery would be allowed to continue where it already existed, but nowhere else in the country. This time the South rejected the proposal.

On March 4, 1861, Lincoln was sworn in as president. In his inaugural address he called for unity. He said that the secession of any state could not be legal, and he called on "the mystic chords of memory" that bound the North and the South.

SHIFTING THE BALANCE

By 1858, the number of free states had for the first time overtaken the number where slavery was allowed. The Crittenden Compromise suggested banning slavery from any states and territories north of Arkansas and west of Missouri.

CHAPTER 4

CONFEDERATE STATES OF AMERICA

The seven states that voted to secede from the Union after the election of President Lincoln formed the Confederate States of America. This, they said, was a new and separate country with its own federal government.

The states took control of federal property within their borders. They sent delegations to Washington, D.C., offering to pay for the federal property they had taken over, and suggesting a peace treaty. Lincoln, however, would not negotiate

The Confederate Battle Flag showed the Southern Cross. It was carried by troops onto the battlefield.

with them. The Confederacy was not a legitimate government, he said. Making a treaty with it would amount to recognizing it as a separate country, and that was something he was not prepared to do.

One-quarter of the U.S. Army was stationed in Texas, and when their commanding general surrendered to state forces they too were handed over. This gave the Confederacy a sizeable armed force. Tension was rising. Lincoln was determined to hold on to the remaining forts in the Confederacy that were occupied by Union forces. These were Fort Monroe in Virginia, Fort Pickens, Fort Jefferson, and Fort Taylor, in Florida, and Fort Sumter in South Carolina.

Not all the slave states chose to leave the Union and join the Confederacy. They were known as the Border States, and they were Delaware, Kentucky, Maryland, and Missouri. West Virginia, which separated from Virginia during the war, was also a Border State. The states of Tennessee, Oklahoma, and Kansas are also sometimes considered Border States. Although these states did not join the Confederacy, there was a mix of support for both the Union and the Confederacy among their populations. Sometimes, communities were so divided that members of the same family fought on opposite sides. Keeping control of these states was important for the Union side when war finally broke out.

KENTUCKY

Kentucky was neutral at the start of the Civil War, but it later joined the Union side. President Lincoln believed it was very important to have the state's support. When speaking about the war he once said that,

"I hope to have God on my side, but I must have Kentucky."

STRONG LEADERS

As war between the Union and Confederate sides became inevitable and drew nearer, the leaders on both sides had a difficult job to do. Both men were strong leaders, driven by their firm belief that right was on their side. There were some striking parallels between their early lives and their entry into politics.

The leader of the Confederacy, the President of the Confederate States of America, was Jefferson Davis. He had been born in Kentucky but grew up in Mississippi, on his family's small farm. He spent some time as a soldier, then a farmer, before he entered politics in 1845. He made an impression with his powerful speeches and his strong belief in the rights of states. When his own state of Mississippi seceded from the Union, in January 1861, he resigned from the Senate and returned home. He accepted the offer of the presidency, even though he would have preferred to serve as a general in the army.

Jefferson Davis was always passionately in favor of the rights of states.

By coincidence, Abraham Lincoln was also born in Kentucky, just eight months after Jefferson Davis and 100 miles (161 km) away. His family was poor and he received little formal education, though he wanted to educate himself and studied hard. He moved to Illinois and worked as a lawyer before he, like Davis, won a seat in Congress in 1845. His arguments against slavery won him national recognition, and he was trusted as an honest politician.

Abraham Lincoln returned to visit his home in Springfield, Illinois, after his election as president in 1860.

HONEST ABE

Abraham Lincoln's nickname was *"Honest Abe."* He was first called this when he was working as a store clerk in Illinois as a young man. He was very careful always to give customers the correct change. His reputation for honesty continued as a lawyer, and made him a popular and trustworthy figure. As president during the Civil War, this reputation made it easy for people to accept his directions, because they believed he was sincere.

THE START OF WAR

Abraham Lincoln was concerned that the armed forces in the federal forts in the Confederacy were effectively in a foreign country. His decision to send them fresh supplies led to the beginning of armed hostilities. The Civil War had begun.

On April 12, Union ships attempted to resupply the Union troops at Fort Sumter in Charleston Harbor, South Carolina. They were fired on by Confederate forces for a punishing 34 hours, and eventually the ships surrendered. The armed forces in the garrison had to surrender, too. Although the Battle of Fort Sumter had no casualties, it marked the beginning of the war.

On April 15, Lincoln called for 75,000 volunteers to join the Northern Army. The states of Virginia, Arkansas, North Carolina, and Tennessee were not willing to contribute men to this new army, and they broke away from the Union. In the end, 3 million men joined the fighting forces on one side or the other. Most of them were volunteers, with only a limited amount of training.

Union forces fire on Fort Sumter in Charleston, South Carolina, after the Confederates attacked it.

In 1861, in the First Battle of Bull Run, the Union Army suffered a heavy defeat.

DEVASTATING WAR

The Civil War devastated the South. Many towns and cities were destroyed, mostly by Union forces under the command of General William T. Sherman (1820–1891), but sometimes by Confederates as they retreated.

Lincoln also announced the Union blockade of Confederate ports. This was designed to stop supplies from either entering or leaving the ports. This weakened the South. The farmers could not get their crops out of the South to sell, so the economy suffered. Just as importantly, vital supplies could not get in, to support the people and the Confederate armed forces.

Soon Richmond, Virginia, was named the new Confederate capital city. The fighting intensified, as many battles were fought during the remainder of 1861, and through 1862. Thousands of soldiers from both sides were killed or wounded. The battles were almost always fought in the Southern states, in both the east and the west. The first was the Battle of Philippi in West Virginia, but this was nothing like as big as the First Battle of Bull Run, fought in Manassass, Virginia, in July 1861, where the Union soldiers were heavily defeated.

CHAPTER 5

THE REALITIES OF WAR

The Civil War was a time of deep divisions, and of great hardship. Not only was the nation divided between Union and Confederate supporters, but local communities, and even families, were divided too. The battles were terrible, and the number of casualties was very high.

It was not uncommon for members of the same family to support opposing sides in the war. This created a lot of bitterness and unhappiness, as families were torn apart. Fathers and their sons might sign up to fight on different sides, or sons might go off to war against the views of their parents. It would take a long time to heal these wounds in families and communities.

As the men went to war, the women were left behind, with little or no source of income. Suddenly they had to take on new responsibilities. Many in the South worked on the family farms, doing hard physical jobs they were unused to, or managing the plantations and their workforce. Another way that women helped was as nurses on the battlefields. There were not enough doctors to treat all the injured soldiers, so their role was a very important one. Medical treatments were still basic in those days, so it was important to clean wounds well to prevent infection spreading. Thousands of women, especially from the North, took on this work. They looked after soldiers on both sides. One woman, named Clara Barton (1821–1912), was known as "The Angel of the Battlefield." After the war she started the American Red Cross.

Rose O'Neal Greenhow (1813–1864) lived in Washington but worked as a spy for the Confederates. She died when her boat sank on a mission to smuggle gold through the Union blockade, in 1864.

Warfare in the 1860s was very different from today. Men fought each other with swords and **bayonets**, and the firearms they had took a long time to reload. Cannons were an important weapon for both sides. They could be used on battlefields and to attack fortifications.

IRONCLAD SHIPS

The Civil War saw the first battle between a new kind of warship, covered with steel armor. They replaced the old wooden ships. In 1862, the USS *Virginia* and the USS *Monitor* met in the Battle of the **Ironclads**.

A DIFFERENT KIND OF WAR

Warfare in the 1860s was very different from today. Men still rode into battle on horseback, and they fought with very different weapons. They were poorly protected against their enemies, and the medical care available for the wounded was very basic. In some ways, however, the Civil War saw the beginnings of new developments in warfare that have continued to today. Transportation and telecommunications, for example, both played important roles.

Civil War soldiers were armed with swords and bayonets. Their firearms, such as muskets, took a long time to reload. A soldier could fire only three shots in 1 minute. During the course of the war, however, improvements were made. By the end of the war there were guns that could fire several shots before needing to be reloaded. Cannons were an important weapon for both sides. They could be used on battlefields against charging troops, and to attack fortifications up to about 3 miles (5 km) away.

More than 175,000 African Americans served in the Union armed forces. Most of them were in the United States Colored Troops regiment. They were paid less than white soldiers. Some white people thought they would not be brave enough to fight, but they were wrong. They fought with great courage and bravery, for example, when they led the Union charge at Fort Wagner, South Carolina, where their action became famous (see page 5). They faced the extra danger of being either sold back into slavery or killed if they were captured by the Confederates.

Unlike modern warfare, some of the "soldiers" on the battlefields were still children. Although the Union set an age limit of 18, about 100,000 boys younger than that signed up to fight. The Confederates had no age limit. Altogether, about 20 percent of the armies on both sides were under the age of 15.

DRUMS

Drums were important during a chaotic battle, to give commands to the troops. The drummers were often young boys. Johnny Clem (1851–1937) joined the Union Army as a drummer boy aged 10. He survived the war and remained in the army until 1915.

The Union Army uniforms of these African American soldiers gave them little protection against the weapons of the enemy.

THE EMANCIPATION PROCLAMATION

On January 1, 1863, President Lincoln issued the Emancipation Proclamation. This declared "that all persons held as slaves" within the rebellious states "are, and henceforward shall be free." This single act changed the legal status of more than 3 million slaves in 10 states of the South, the states still in rebellion: Texas,

This was the first reading of the Emancipation Proclamation to the cabinet, in July 1862. President Lincoln is third from the left.

South Carolina, North Carolina, Georgia, Alabama, Mississippi, Arkansas, Virginia, Kentucky, and Louisiana. As soon as slaves could escape from a Confederate area, they became a free person.

As the Union forces advanced into Confederate states, they began to free thousands of slaves every day. Many slaves did not wait for the Union Army to reach them, they ran away from their owners to claim their freedom. About 4 million slaves in these states were eventually freed. Some of them joined the Union Army, to fight their former owners.

The Proclamation did not take effect in the Border States, which were not at war with the Union. Before the war was over, some of them ended slavery within their territories. The Proclamation was important because it showed clearly that the aim of the Union was no longer only to reunite the country as one nation. They also had a clear aim to abolish slavery.

Although the Proclamation freed slaves, it did not make slavery illegal. Lincoln therefore set about making this happen. He proposed an amendment to the Constitution that would ban slavery. This, the Thirteenth Amendment, was finally passed late in 1865, a few months after Lincoln was **assassinated**.

THE BORDER STATES

President Lincoln waited until January 1863 to issue the Emancipation Proclamation, because he needed to know first, and most importantly, that he could win the war. To win, he needed the support of the Border States, and many people living in them did not support the abolition of slavery. Only when it was clear that the Union could win was it safe to free the slaves.

KEY EVENTS

These are some of the key dates in the history of this complex and long conflict.

1850

September 18 The Fugitive Slave Act is passed by Congress.

1854

May 30 The Kansas-Nebraska Act becomes law.

1860

November 6 Abraham Lincoln is elected President of the United States.

December 20 South Carolina officially secedes from the Union.

1861

February 8–9 The Confederate States of America is formed, with Jefferson Davis as President.

March 4 Abraham Lincoln is inaugurated as U.S. President.

April 17 The state of Virginia votes to leave the Union.

1862

March 8–9 The Battle of the Ironclads.

1863

January 1 Abraham Lincoln issues the Emancipation Proclamation.

July 1–3 The Battle of Gettysburg.

November 19 Abraham Lincoln delivers the Gettysburg Address.

1864

June 28 Abraham Lincoln repeals the fugitive slave laws.

1865

January 31 The U.S. Congress passes the Thirteenth Amendment, abolishing slavery.

April 9 Robert E. Lee (1807–1870), Confederate commander, surrenders to Union commander, Ulysses S. Grant (1822–1885).

April 14 Abraham Lincoln is shot. He dies the next day.

June 2 The war ends when the Confederate port of Galveston, in Texas, finally surrenders.

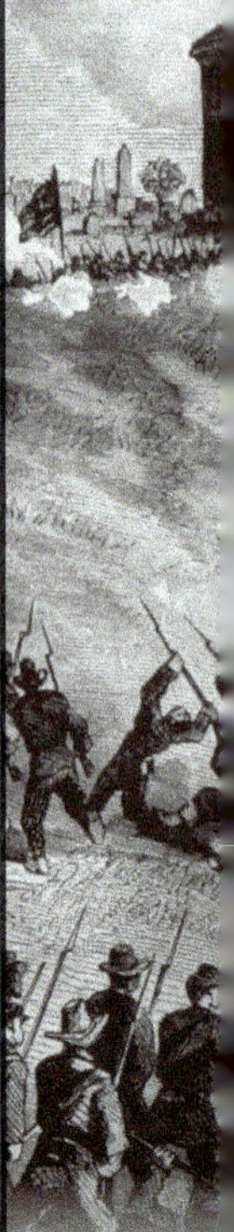

GETTYSBURG

The Battle of Gettysburg (below), in Pennsylvania, was a turning point in the war, as it ended the Confederate attempt to invade the North. At the ceremony to open the cemetery for Union soldiers killed in the battle, Lincoln delivered the Gettysburg Address. He called for *"a new birth of freedom"* in the nation, so that *"the government of the people, by the people, and for the people shall not perish from the Earth."*

CHAPTER 6

END OF THE WAR AND ITS LEGACY

By 1865, both sides were exhausted by four years of war. The Confederates were losing. The Union Army had begun marching through Virginia, pushing back the Confederates.

General Robert E. Lee of the Confederate Army was forced to abandon the capital, Richmond. He and his troops came to a halt at Appomattox, Virginia. They were surrounded, and greatly outnumbered. On April 9, General Lee and the Union's General Ulysses S. Grant met to discuss the terms of a surrender. General Grant had discussed this already with President Lincoln. It was important to reach a deal that would bring an end to the war once and for all. Lincoln did not want Confederate soldiers to start rebelling again if the terms were too harsh. It was agreed that the soldiers would turn in their weapons, but they could keep their horses and return home. There would be no prisoners or punishments. This was a fair deal, and General Lee had to accept it. When other Confederate forces heard of Lee's surrender, they did the same. President Davis was captured, however, and he spent two years in prison.

Just a few days later, tragedy struck. President Lincoln was assassinated in Washington, D.C., while at the theater. His killer was John Wilkes Booth (1838–1865), who was soon killed during the attempt to capture him. Booth had hoped to revive the Confederacy, and after Lincoln's death the president's plans for a speedy and peaceful reunion of the nation would be severely challenged. On April 26, Vice President Andrew Johnson (1808–1875) was sworn in as the new president.

In the South, people started trying to put their lives back together. This was a huge task, as so many had been killed and wounded, and so much property had been destroyed. Some communities had lost almost their entire male population.

The city of Richmond in Virginia was in ruins by 1865. These slaves would have been recently freed.

NATIONAL CEMETERIES

Before the Civil War there were no national cemeteries to bury and remember the dead from military conflicts. In 1864, Arlington National Cemetery, Virginia, was established as the first one. In 1867, Congress set up a program to rebury Union soldiers in 74 national cemeteries, though Confederate soldiers were not included in the plan.

RECONSTRUCTION

The period from 1865, when the war ended, to 1877 is known as the Reconstruction Era. This was the time when the government tried to reconstruct the South, and to create a united nation once again. The politicians were going to find it tough to bring the former Confederate states back into the Union.

Abraham Lincoln had wanted to avoid conflict as much as possible in reconciling with the Southern states, and the new President Johnson agreed with his plan. In fact, he wanted to be even more lenient, as he was from the South himself. Unfortunately, there were others in the government who held a different view. They wanted the Confederates to be punished for trying to leave the Union. They were called the Radical Republicans. Another policy they wanted to introduce was giving equal rights to African Americans. This included giving them the right to vote in elections. President Johnson and the Radical Republicans came into conflict many times over the following years, and Congress began to pass harsh laws for Southern states.

Gradually, new governments were formed in the South. The first state to rejoin the Union was Tennessee, in 1866, and the last was Georgia, in 1870. All states being readmitted had to ratify, or agree to, three new amendments to the Constitution. These were: the Thirteenth Amendment that outlawed slavery; the Fourteenth Amendment that declared that black and white people should be treated equally in law as citizens of the United States; and the Fifteenth Amendment that gave everyone the right to vote, regardless of their race.

The Union spent money to rebuild the South. They rebuilt roads and schools, and helped farmers get their farms running again. Gradually, the economy began to recover. The Reconstruction ended under President Rutherford B. Hayes (1822–1893) in 1877, when he removed the last federal troops from the South.

CIVIL RIGHTS

The new amendments to the Constitution helped advance **civil rights** and equality between people of different race or color, but they did not solve the problems of racial injustice. Many of the changes to equal rights introduced during Reconstruction were reversed by the new Southern governments.

Benjamin Sterling Turner (1825–1894) was born a slave, but he was educated. After the Civil War he entered politics in Alabama and he was elected to the House of Representatives in 1870.

MODERN PROGRESS

The Civil War was a war about slavery. If there had been no disagreement between North and South over the issue of slavery, the conflict would not have started. The South would not have felt that its way of life was under threat, and would not have tried to leave the Union.

In the 1960s, many African Americans joined marches like this one, protesting their segregation in education and housing, and demanding an end to discrimination.

It was not just a war about slavery, however. Many Southerners were much more interested in being able to preserve their culture and their way of life, free from interference from the North. Therefore, the other big issue at the heart of the war was the rights of states to determine their own affairs, and whether or not it was possible for them to leave the Union. This was an argument about the U.S. Constitution.

The unequal treatment of African Americans did certainly not end in the South after the war was over. The new governments passed laws to keep blacks and whites segregated and unequal in all areas of daily life. These were known as the Jim Crow laws. In the 1950s and 1960s, the Civil Rights movement set out to change this culture of inequality for African Americans. Their methods were peaceful and included marches and protests, but their message was powerful. Many people, such as their leader Martin Luther King, Jr., risked their lives for the cause. In 1964, the Civil Rights Act finally made it illegal to discriminate against people based on their race, color, gender, national origin, or religion. More progress has been made toward equality since then.

The Civil War had a lasting impact on the country. It took a long time for the wounds to heal, and even longer for the whole nation to learn the lesson of equality for all. Today, African Americans play an equal part in the life of the nation, and are free to rise to the highest offices in the land.

MEMORIAL DAY

The Civil War is commemorated every year on Memorial Day, when we remember the sacrifices made by those who fought on both sides.

GLOSSARY

abolitionists people in favor of abolishing slavery and making it illegal

agriculture the science or practice of growing crops and raising animals

assassinated deliberately killed

bayonets sharp knives attached to the front ends of rifles for use in combat

casualties people who are injured or killed in an accident or a war

civil rights the rights of people to freedom and equality

civil war a war fought between two sides from the same country

compromise a way of avoiding conflict by giving up something to reach agreement

discrimination treating people differently because of their race, gender, or religion

economy the wealth and resources of a country or region

emancipation gaining freedom

immigrants people who move to another country to live and work

ironclads ships covered with iron or steel to protect them from shot

plantations very large farms—usually in hot regions—where crops, such as cotton, are grown

resources supplies of something necessary or valuable that can be used when required

secede to withdraw from a group or a country

slaves people who are sold to other people to work and lose their freedom

treason the betrayal of your country

U.S. Constitution a document first adopted in 1788, which explains the different parts of the U.S. government and the basic rights of citizens

FOR MORE INFORMATION

BOOKS

Bearce, Stephanie. *The Civil War: Spies, Secret Missions, and Hidden Facts from the Civil War* (Top Secret Files). Waco, TX: Prufrock Press, 2014.

Civil War (DK Eyewitness). New York, NY: Dorling Kindersley, 2015.

Thompson, Ben. *The American Civil War* (Guts & Glory). New York, NY: Little, Brown Books for Young Readers, 2015.

WEBSITES

Take a look at the huge variety of Civil War articles, maps, and videos at:

www.civilwar.org/education/history

Click through the links for information on the major events, battles, and people involved in the Civil War at:

www.ducksters.com/history/civil_war.php

Visit this website for a comprehensive look at the history of African Americans in the United States at:

www.history.com/topics/black-history

INDEX